3.00

D1197194

Take Back
Your Weekends

Allison Graham

©2021 Allison Graham
Elevate Seminars and Strategic Development Inc.
AllisonGraham.co

All rights reserved. No part of this work covered by the copyright herein may be reproduced or used in any form or by any means – graphic, electronic or mechanical – without the prior written permission of the publisher.

This publication contains the opinions and ideas of its author and is designed to provide useful advice in regard to the subject matter covered. The author and publisher are not engaged in rendering medical, therapeutic, or other services in this publication. This publication is not intended to provide a basis for action in particular circumstances without consideration by a competent professional. The author and publisher expressly disclaim any responsibility for any liability, loss or risk, personal or otherwise, which is incurred as a consequence, directly or indirectly, of the use and application of any of the contents of this book.

Library and Archives Canada Cataloguing in Publication
Graham, Allison Dawn, 1975—
Take Back Your Weekends / Allison Graham
Issued in print, electronic and audio formats

Publisher:
Elevate Press
305-611 Wonderland Road North
London ON, N6H 5N7
Canada

eBook ISBN: 9780981062365 | paperback ISBN: 9780981062372

WHAT IF YOU WORKED WITHOUT DESTRUCTIVE STRESS?

I was mid-way through a workshop with a small executive team. One of the leaders started to cry.

He said, "I'm scared I'll miss my kids' childhood. I spend every Saturday and Sunday working. It's still not enough."

That was the first time I said, "Well, take back your weekends!" It was not the last time.

Some people love working long hours. I won't say that's bad. That'd be hypocritical – I love to work!

Instead, my goal is to show you how to feel less stressed while you work. I want you to have the choice to enjoy free time and fully relax when you do.

If working all weekend makes you happy – go for it.

If, like many others, you want more downtime, then you're about to uncover a new freedom from your to-do list.

The time-thieves that cause destructive stress are waiting to be uncovered. Remove these from your work week and watch your outputs per hour soar.

You'll no longer have to work weekends to make up for stolen hours during the typical nine to five. Then you can choose how to spend your found time.

Privately leaders share with me that they're frustrated, overwhelmed and discouraged. Many won't admit this to their peers for fear of being judged.

Well, there is zero judgment from me. I fully accept that each of us has a behind-the-scenes story. Many leaders say their plates are full. There always seems to be too much to do, with too little time and too few resources.

Add to the mix multiple priorities, team dynamics, life's hard knocks and a pandemic. It's no wonder burnout and stress leave are at an all-time high.

With a few small tweaks to your workday, this spinning in the vortex of stress can stop!

Humans weren't built for long-term stress. Research has proven that sustained, unmanaged stress can lead to health challenges and a lower quality of life.

We need downtime to recover. When we work for hours on end, even when we're on a roll, performance can dwindle. The body's need to reset is neglected in pursuit of goals.

Rest contributes to achieving bigger goals more easily and living a more enjoyable life.

For some, the 24/7 hustle works. For others, like me, buying into the busy-is-best culture kept me from feeling a sense of peace and happiness.

My life felt out of my control.

Being busy was a way of life. I thought the "hustle" was a mandatory part of success. Every few weeks I'd collapse from exhaustion; then get back to the grind.

Life was a blur. Underneath the hustle, I was unhappy.

I worried about everything that had to get done. I felt guilty about what I wasn't doing. Rarely did I stop to celebrate my achievements.

I overloaded my schedule with work and volunteer activities. I served everyone else's agenda, while rarely taking time for my own needs.

Does any of this sound familiar in your life?

Another issue was that I didn't know how to ride waves of grief, heartbreak and physical pain. Looking back, I realize that I stayed busy to avoid feeling life's hardest emotions.

That pace was not sustainable. Ultimately, I was forced to course correct. I needed a less stressful way to succeed.

My 18-hour workdays came to a screeching halt after a surgical complication. Physical pain and unrealistic expectations to do too much forced me to stop.

I traded long hours for a handful of hours of functionality each day for many years. Rest was no longer a luxury; it was non-negotiable.

Everything about how I worked was on the table. The goal was to find a way to build my company and expand my personal brand in fewer hours, without stress.

I studied every self-help modality I could find. I spent eight years working with a psychologist who specialized in chronic pain. A lot of my frameworks have been shaped by this experience with Cognitive Behavioural Therapy.

At times, I think I was more productive and effective when I had limited capacity each day.

Now that I work full-time again, I continually leverage the ideas in this book to avoid burnout, while actively growing my speaking and consulting business.

As I talk with professionals from around the globe, I realize that the way I was living is quite typical. Many seem to relate to the frustration of the expected hustle.

Many don't realize they are caught in the vortex of stress and that's why they lack joy in the day-to-day.

They long for a sense of peace, fulfilment and happiness, but they don't know how to achieve it or even if they can.

It absolutely is possible. There is light at the end of the tunnel, even if you can't see it yet!

I learned that the answers to a more fulfilling, less stressful life are found outside of the busy-busy-go-go-go.

It may be uncomfortable, at least it was for me, but the perspective needed for true growth and change is waiting "inside the stop."

Pausing to take an objective look at how we respond to the circumstances swirling around us is essential to changing unhealthy patterns.

A proactive approach to address both mindset and methods is needed for meaningful impact.

If you're ready to take control of your time, then I invite you to join me in discovering a better, less stressful way to do all that you do.

The results will lead to even higher quality work outputs, better mental health and stronger connections with the people you love.

Let this book be your "stop." Now is your chance to course correct before life forces you to stop. It's time to Take Back Your Weekends! ▪

COACHING QUESTIONS

Do you find yourself working weekends, late nights or early mornings to complete unfinished work?

What does Take Back Your Weekends mean to you and why is it important to you? What will you do with your new-found time freedom?

Are you truly relaxed during non-work time? Do lingering to-dos play on your mind, blocking the potential for feeling refreshed?

Can you relate to any elements of my story? If so, which ones?

Write your stress story. Create a snapshot of your life now and what you want to change.

FINDING A PATH TO FREE TIME

—

To Take Back Your Weekends here are three options:

1. Work longer hours during the week.
2. Stop doing some of the tasks you're doing.
3. Change the way you approach the work you do.

Let's discuss each.

Working longer hours during the week would defeat the goal of this book – to find more downtime. More hours at work during the week will add to your risk of burnout. Let's skip option one.

Option two has a lot of merit and requires thorough analysis. Explore what you're doing and if you must, in fact, be doing it.

This can lead down a rabbit hole of self-awareness.

Even though I love navigating that discovery process with clients, it's too individualized an experience for this book.

If you choose to explore option two on your own, and I hope you do, here are some questions to consider:

- Do you lack boundaries and say yes instead of no?
- Do you feel obligated to pick up the slack for others?
- Does "doing it all" win you approval, yours or others?
- Is there a reason you resist delegating?
- Is your identity too closely aligned with being busy?

See? Rabbit hole.

Then there's option three. Change the way you approach your work. You and I are about to go deep into this topic.

It doesn't require a complicated overhaul of your entire work environment. It's easy with a little insight and practice.

This book is not another productivity hack to get organized. A better system to manage your to-do list won't liberate days each month.

Yes, it's essential to have an organized task-tracking system. Later in this book, I share the absolute best way I've found for my clients and me to manage tasks.

It's also covered in depth in the third section of my *Take Back Your Weekends* online course.

It's clear that a new task system is not the answer because if it was, you wouldn't be reading this book. Most successful professionals have tried every productivity program on the market. I did.

Still, they're frustrated. Clients have come to me after spending thousands of dollars searching for remedies.

Instead, my approach is to uncover the subtle nuances that steal productivity.

To make real, lasting change, you need a new relationship with stress. Then you can leverage good stress and minimize typical destructive stress.

Time freedom is found by shifting how you allocate your emotional, mental and physical capacity each day toward tasks, obstacles and adversities.

The key is to remove hidden, seemingly innocent time-sucks from your workdays. For example, eliminating fanfare around tasks and problem-solving can unlock hours each week.

You've likely seen this in action.

A little worry here; some procrastination there. Too many interruptions here; a lack of focus there.

Each is a barrier to performance that contributes to the overflowing workload and overtime requirements.

Sure, there will be crunch times when you absolutely have to work extra hours. That's when you rally for an intense sprint, but It isn't sustainable.

Many live in hope of the illusive "one day" when the pace will slow and stress will disappear, as if by magic.

My hope is you can remove the destructive stress reaction even with today's circumstances - no magic required.

For years, one of my best friends said, "Things are really busy right now. When they slowdown, I'll write my book."

She's said that for as long as I can remember. The busy hasn't stopped. The book and her other passion projects haven't been started.

For years she's not lived her joy because of being busy.

The hardest part has been watching her be frustrated and stressed for years, knowing that there is a better, less stressful way!

When you interrupt patterns that steal time needlessly, you'll be exponentially more productive.

By default, it'll be easy to Take Back Your Weekends! ■

COACHING QUESTIONS

Are there projects or activities that you have not had time to do in your life because you're too busy?

Do you have regular crunch times in your work or is every day a crunch time?

Of the three ways to Take Back Your Weekends, which is most appealing to you and why?

Please answer the questions outlined on Page 14 to explore the second option to Take Back Your Weekends, which was to stop doing some of the tasks you're doing.

Have you tried various productivity systems over the years? What's worked, what hasn't?

MY PROBLEM-SOLVING FRAMEWORK

—

Typically, when we face a challenge, we immediately look for a solution. It feels logical, but solution-first thinking is not the best way to solve problems.

Think about it like this...

- You already know one solution to time management is to delegate; yet perhaps you're someone who resists.
- You know you need to do important tasks first. Still, days fly by. Priorities get pushed again and again.
- You know procrastination kills productivity. You want to "just do it." Still, dreaded tasks linger.
- You know worrying denies daily happiness and you need to "stop it." Yet, the imagination runs wild.

See, if knowing the solution meant we implemented the solution, we'd all be perfect. We're not.

Yet, we are extraordinarily capable of shifting patterns.

Dieting is an obvious example of how solution-first thinking doesn't solve problems effectively.

Someone decides to lose weight and chooses a diet. On day one they're eager. By day five they're eating nachos, drinking beer and watching a Netflix marathon.

It doesn't mean the person is doomed to never lose weight. They can, just not by jumping to solution first.

To interrupt unhelpful patterns that have been reinforced for decades, we first need to go to the heart of the issue. Then solutions have a fighting chance to stick.

For example, before writing this book, I wrote a guide with the *Top 21 Tips to Take Control of Your Time.*

It's full of great strategies. Yet, I've decided not to release it as a standalone product.

Why? Because without the foundational thinking shared in this book, the solutions won't be as successful.

Instead, the guide will be available for readers who have finished this book and students who have registered for my full Take Back Your Weekends online program. To access these tips, please go to TakeBackYourWeekends.com

Unless you *shift your thinking* about time management, the long hours of work won't change. Imagine working weekends for the rest of your career.

Would that cause you regret?

This is where my 3-part problem-solving framework comes into play.

My problem-solving framework starts with Situational Awareness. This is a method to evaluate the issues at hand.

Understanding this will open possibilities for less stress.

My clients have found that having a common language to address tasks, obstacles and adversities is a powerful tool to improve communication and perspective.

The second part of my problem-solving framework is Self-Awareness. This is where we reflect on how you're responding to challenges.

As part of this step, we explore how your reaction may make an issue more difficult or a task more cumbersome. Look for anything that unnecessarily drains capacity.

The third part of the framework is Solution Activation. This is easier after completing parts one and two. Pausing to create an informed perspective leads to the best solutions.

This framework and its supporting components are a way of thinking about challenges and changes. It gives you and your team a systematic way to tackle problems.

This process can be applied to any issue you face.

It could be something as important as fixing your family's morning routine or as complex as solving this quarter's revenue dip. You could use it to streamline operations.

In my coaching practice, I use it to help clients lower stress and cut through the noise when they're overwhelmed.

Personally I use the framework anytime I feel out of flow or have a problem to solve.

The framework is designed to shift your stress response from destructive to empowered in a matter of minutes.

For this book, we'll apply my problem-solving framework to your heavy workload that spills into your weekends.

Since you don't want to take back ONE weekend, we need to use all three parts of the framework.

To get one weekend off, just say "Screw it!" and turn off your phone for a couple of days.

Unfortunately, without the tweak to your work week, you'll pay for that choice. You'll be even further behind.

The true goal is to get your weekends – with an "S" – back within your control.

You may choose to work on the weekends - you may not.

The point is to have the choice.

In future chapters, I'll share more about my Problem-Solving framework. First, it's important to cover some supporting concepts. These will help guide your journey to Take Back Your Weekends. ▪

COACHING QUESTIONS

Can you think of an example in your life where you've jumped to solution-first thinking?

Have you ever found a solution to an obstacle, but it didn't stick for the long term?

If you never take back your weekends, time or power, would that cause you regret in your life? How so?

INVEST TIME TODAY TO BUY BACK TIME TOMORROW

Remember I said, "in the stop we find the best answers." As the old saying goes, slow down to speed up.

Investing time to read this book is a wise decision. I'm guessing you realize that if you don't do something differently, you'll get more of the same results.

It's time to take back your time. It is actually quite simple. There's lost time hiding everywhere and it's waiting for you to claim it!

As mentioned earlier, your solution doesn't have to be a massive overhaul of your working environment. You need to find those subtle nuances to achieve time freedom.

Small tweaks yield big results.

The goal is to buy back ten minutes here, 30 minutes here and another two minutes there. Combined, these small wins over four or five workdays are significant.

For example, what if you cut default meeting length by half company-wide? Too much? Start with a 10 or 20% reduction. Consider booking 20 minutes instead of 30 minutes. Instead of one hour, book 50 minutes.

People ask me, "How long after taking this program will it be until I genuinely feel control over my time?"

Well, it depends. That's entirely up to you.

Some people see results in a day. Others take weeks or months to shift. Some <u>choose</u> to stay stuck.

There are several pieces to the puzzle. It's like anything. What you put in determines what you get out.

One indication is a person's willingness to objectively explore their patterns, without judging themselves. This is not about being wrong or right. It's about choosing to walk through life in a way that minimizes your stress response.

Clients find these concepts easy to implement once they're understood. It shifts their fundamental thinking about stress and everything they have to do.

If you want to go even further with these concepts, you have options. I offer speaking and coaching programs as well as the full *Take Back Your Weekends online* course.

My in-depth training program is called the *Rapid-Fire Resilience Rundown*.

In the program, over several weeks, teams discover a system that guides them from challenge to effective solution. It's essentially a critical-thinking checklist to use any time you feel overwhelmed or face a challenge.

For now, in this book, my goal is to give you enough knowledge to get you started, so you can successfully Take Back Your Weekends.

When I've studied other productivity frameworks, I've felt overwhelmed. It took hours to read the books. That's why I've made this a short read that's simple to digest.

Other systems often require complicated implementation strategies and software. Mine doesn't.

All you need is a pen and paper. That, plus some perseverance and a willingness to find the small tweaks that will lead to the big results you desire.

The time you'll invest to read this book will ultimately save you hundreds of hours in the future. ▪

COACHING QUESTIONS

How many hours do you want to free from your work week and your weekends?

Do you feel a sensation of resistance to anything I've written so far? If so, that's excellent data to bring to your awareness. Please acknowledge it and consider exploring it further.

Before we dive into how to uncover those hidden hours, is there anything in your week that is an obvious time suck that you can identify?

LET'S TALK ABOUT YOUR TO-DO LIST

—

About five minutes into my first call with a new coaching client the tears started.

Sidebar. You may notice that professionals cry around me a lot. It means they feel safe to have a breakthrough. My goal is for clients to leave our sessions feeling hopeful and inspired to take action and step into their brilliance.

My client's tears were from frustration.

When she works, she feels guilty that she's not spending time with her family.

When she's relaxing, she feels guilty because she knows the work is piling even higher.

It's a vicious cycle.

"I just can't get caught up. It's impossible," she cried.

YES. EXACTLY.

A to-do list doesn't end. The finish line always moves. A task comes off the list - another task, two or ten, get added. Chasing its completion is a game you can't win.

It's not a list. It's a Task Circle. It just keeps going.

The fact that the tasks never end is a good thing. If they did, you'd be out of a job, bored out of your mind or both.

The tasks to be done are not actually the problem. It's the negative emotional and mental connection to the unfinished tasks that's the problem.

The sooner you detach from the expectation that everything must get done right now, the sooner you can Take Back Your Weekends.

If your to-do list influences your mood your happiness is at risk. You'll waste time judging yourself harshly or feeling guilty that you aren't doing enough.

Don't let incomplete items steal hours of enjoyment and contentment from your life.

Seriously, how can you relax and enjoy time with family and friends when you feel guilty about the unfinished list?

I get it. The list calls to you. *I'm here, you're ignoring me. Please, come back. If you ignore me, you're a failure.*

Blah, blah, blah.

I'm challenging you to emotionally and mentally detach from your to-do list.

How?

First, by recognizing your connection to the to-do list. Explore the emotions and storyline around it.

Are you judging yourself unfairly? Is your mood influenced by how well your list is managed?

Next, realize that the list is just the place where all the tasks you could do are captured.

The purpose of the list is to free your mental capacity. Once a task is on your list, technically you do not need to think about it again until it's time to focus on that task.

Think of the countless thinking-hours you've lost going over tasks in your head. *I've got to do this, I've got to do that, and this, and that, and OMG what if I forget that?*

Why waste mental energy worrying about what has to be done?

Thinking about the fact that you have to do an item that is already captured on your list is double dipping.

Either it's your brain's responsibility to remember a task or it's your list's responsibility. Not both. Write it and forget it.

It's different if you use thinking time to be creative. Time spent contemplating how to effectively do something on your list is part of the innovation process.

If you're not capturing tasks in an effective way, this is definitely something to consider. The people I've worked with who don't have an efficient task-tracking system, tend to be more stressed than those who do.

A lot of professionals say their mind goes into hyper drive when their head hits their pillow. That's when a lot of task-remembering and mental-list-making starts.

When that happens it's a double whammy. Not only do you have too much to do; you're extra tired from not sleeping thanks to thinking of everything you have to do.

See how unproductive that is?

I tried to remember pillow-thoughts. The effort kept me from falling asleep.

Getting a quality night's sleep is complex. Creating mental lists makes it harder. The way I fixed the issue was simple.

I keep a pen and paper on my night stand. Instead of trying to remember, I scribble the idea on the paper.

After a thought is on paper it's released from my brain. It takes mental discipline to trust the paper to hold the thought, but with practice it is possible.

The list is more reliable than the brain when it comes to remembering tasks to be done.

Trust the paper. Get the sleep. ▪

COACHING QUESTIONS

Is your mood influenced by how well you're managing your to-do list? In what ways?

Do you trust your task-tracking system or does remembering tasks drain your capacity?

Challenge yourself to write it and forget it.

Do you have trouble shutting off your work brain when you want to relax or are trying to fall asleep?

GOOD VERSUS DESTRUCTIVE STRESS

—

Not all stress is bad. In fact, stress-done-right can be a highly effective tool to drive your success.

Stress plays vital roles in our lives. We're alive thanks to stress. Without it, predators would have eaten us long ago.

Stress hormones spike in a moment of danger. That's our cue to run to safety.

Once safe, hormones are supposed to settle. We're designed to return to our neutral baseline.

Stress turns destructive when it's sustained for long periods without returning to baseline. People spend way too much of their lives with stress hormones firing in high gear.

Another way stress switches from being helpful to a hindrance is when stress hormones fire as if there is danger when there is no real danger in sight.

Imaginary danger is responsible for a lot of unnecessary stress. A heavy workload and other obstacles that come with success and living a full life are not the same as predators.

If there's a constant battle with these daily realities, the stress hormones fire as if the tigers are hunting the person.

Eventually that causes a stress-related problem like burnout, lost work outputs or dialling it in on the job.

When it's time to relax, people are so exhausted from the sustained intensity of running from perceived tigers, leisure feels more like a collapse than a recharge.

Repeat after me: "My to-do list is not a predator."

Destructive stress also can develop when barriers to performance such as worrying, blaming, allowing constant interruptions and negativity are added to daily tasks and obstacles. More on that in future chapters.

Science tells us that the risk of prolonged, unmanaged workplace stress is directly linked to disease.

Long before disease from chronic stress strikes, there are a host of frustrating consequences. For example, a lack of joy and enthusiasm each day.

In healthy doses and with the right approach, stress can be very positive. In fact, it can be what inspires you to reach for goals and focuses you to achieve them.

It's a balancing act.

Too much stress and you're operating on the cusp of burnout. Nothing good and productive happens when your emotional, mental and physical capacities are maxed.

Too little stress and you're going to feel unchallenged. Accomplished professionals need to stretch themselves to be in flow.

Imagine stress levels on a scale from one to ten, with one being absolute boredom and ten being absolutely frazzled.

Somewhere on that scale, perhaps around a four, five, six, or maybe a seven, is your sweet spot of performance, productivity and profitability. You can find it at the intersection of a goal, a deadline and accountability.

This optimal zone is not possible in a prolonged state. We can't spend every moment chasing goals and deadlines.

The intensity of activity needs to vary from high-focus to low-focus to make this work. The recharge which happens at the lower end of the stress scale, is required to accelerate for another round of intensity.

An hour of highly productive, uninterrupted, completely focused work two or three times per day produces greater outputs than eight hours of non-focused, out-of-flow work.

Many professionals go through workdays putting out fires and reacting to outside influences. They never get focused bursts. Then, they are forced to work weekends to compensate for the lost productivity.

It's easy to get pulled in different directions by other people's agendas or distractions.

- Well, I guess that can wait.
- Sure, I'll do this trivial task not the one that matters.
- You want to interrupt me, why not, let's chat.
- Hello shiny, blinky thing.

Sidebar. One day I was writing a Linked In post about productivity and caught myself being mesmerized by a squirrel outside my window. The irony was not lost on me. I snapped a pic. To catch my latest musings and other content, follow me on Linked In: allisongraham.co/linkedin

To completely eliminate natural distractions from the workday is unrealistic. I believe it's best to embrace human nature and accentuate our natural rhythms.

Even the busiest professionals, if committed, can carve several highly productive sprints throughout the work week.

These bursts of total focus were the key to my success. It was especially important when nerve pain meant I only had a few hours to work each day.

Initially, I didn't realize why. I wondered how I could trade 18-hour days for a handful of hours and accomplish more important tasks and grow my business.

The answer: by sky-rocketing my output per hour. This allowed me to take as much downtime as I needed.

This see-saw method of being focused then taking a break naturally occurred in my life because I had no choice.

I accidentally harnessed good stress to maximize outputs in a shorter amount of time.

- I had a goal - to keep my business alive.
- I had a deadline - before the pain forced me to stop.
- I had accountability – expectations from a client, media outlet or the bank gave me the motivation I needed.

You've likely experienced zones of massive productivity, too. Quite possibly on weekends, late at night or early in the morning, when you don't really want to work, but you must.

It's in these crunch times that projects get done faster. You have one directive for the time allocated. "I'm going to get caught up on X."

Plus, you have a deadline to get it done and perhaps someone's expectation that you'll finish by a certain time. *"Honey, you said you were only going to work till noon."* tugs on the heartstrings.

Once it's understood that good stress can inspire and focus, that knowledge can be used to design your life.

The goal is to add these bursts of flow state into every workday. That'll get "off-hours" productivity built into the regular work hours.

When you carve more opportunities to operate in your sweet spot of performance, productivity and profitability during the week, by default, you'll have freedom to Take Back Your Weekends! ▪

COACHING QUESTIONS

How much of your time is spent in a stressed state?

Are you currently noticing any stress-induced problems in your life? What are they? How are they impacting your life?

How often are you getting into a flow state for your work? What does it feel like?

What types of distractions do you face each day that take you away from your flow state?

Are you active on Linked In? If so, please connect. I'd love to hear your answers. A direct link to my profile is: allisongraham.co/linkedin

LEVERAGING STRESS

—

At the risk of jumping ahead to Solution Activation, I want to share a framework with you to incorporate good stress into your work week.

Later I'll share more about the Task Circle Method which is all about leveraging good stress and alternating it with rest.

For now, let's focus on the importance of getting the three aspects of good stress to intersect. That's where you'll find your Sweet Spot of Performance, Productivity and Profitability.

Ideally find several periods of continuous and intense effort that include a goal, deadline and accountability. Follow those bursts of focus with a lower-focus activity to reset.

These can be called work blocks, bursts, sprints, focused effort, pomodoros or any other phrase you choose. The words are interchangeable, the concept remains the same.

5 Steps To Add Focused Work Bursts To Your Week:

1. Choose two or three time slots per day for focused work blocks. (45 – 75 minutes each. I'll explain why later.)
2. Protect that time.
3. Determine a clear goal for each work block.
4. Set a deadline.
5. Build in accountability.

The challenge that I hear from most professionals who work in a team or schedule back-to-back meetings all day is that there is no space for these focused work bursts.

"But Allison, I can't get uninterrupted time."

Yes, you can. You choose not to set boundaries to get it.

A good friend failed to take vacations for several years. Finally, she met with her leadership team and said, "To better serve you I need time away – I need you to respect my vacation. Do not call."

The team was supportive.

Now, she takes refreshing, uninterrupted vacations. So does everyone on the team.

The same conversation about boundaries works at the day-to-day level, too.

I love working with teams to create systems so that each person gets time for focused work in their sweet spot of performance, productivity and profitability.

The strategy to find time blocks is easier than you may think when the whole team is on side.

Have the conversation about what it takes for each person to find their optimal zone.

Embed this commitment to focused effort into your culture and communications. Put it on the shared calendar.

Empower each person to set boundaries and expectations to protect their sprints.

Unless it's a legitimate fire, interruptions are not allowed.

Some teams choose to do their bursts at the same time. Then no one is available to cause interruptions.

Once you set your time blocks, determine what you're going to accomplish in each.

Setting stretch goals is an excellent way to jolt yourself into high gear.

When you strive for big or small goals, it charts a clear path of where to spend your time. Suddenly, unimportant, distracting tasks lose their appeal.

No goal = no priority = no focus = lost productivity

Each day set your priorities and then design meetings and work blocks accordingly.

But Allison, I don't have BIG goals. I just have to get through the mundane stuff on my desk.

YES, exactly. Make that your goal. Same principles apply.

A caution. For us to be inspired to achieve a big goal, we need to take small, consistent steps.

If satisfaction is only tied to achieving big goals, you may wait weeks, months or even years to feel accomplished.

Get emotionally fired-up by completing small milestones to gain momentum. When you fall in love with the day-to-day pursuits and the seemingly insignificant steps along the way it's easier to find joy and happiness.

Split big projects into the smallest tasks you can define.

It's empowering to mark small tasks completed. Once combined, the small tasks will make accomplishing the big project inevitable.

If you have ten minutes before your next meeting, you can do a small task to contribute to the big project.

The satisfaction that comes from achieving a goal within the dedicated work block can motivate you to do another.

Having a deadline for any activity is imperative.

It's Parkinson's Law - work expands to fill the time allotted.

I love the sharpened focus from deadlines.

My first newspaper column was published August 15th, 2003. I was so nervous. Instead of enjoying the start of an incredible journey, I was completely stressed in anticipation of my submission deadline.

As the years passed, with four columns a week under my belt, I learned how to manage the pressure of deadlines.

My deadline was 3:00PM. In the early days, I'd start writing first thing in the morning or the day before. I'd submit on time; rarely early. The column consumed most of my day.

A few times life got in the way. I couldn't start writing until 2:00PM. It was fascinating to me that, with only an hour to write, I still submitted my work on time.

That's good stress in action. Deadline looms. The brain becomes hyper-focused. The work gets done faster.

Deadlines backfire when planned poorly. Good stress quickly turns to bad when there's not enough time.

For example, if I started writing at 2:45PM, I would submit late. I couldn't produce a publishable column in 15 minutes.

Booking back-to-back meetings all day is a form of deadline overload that will backfire.

You can't end a meeting at 1:00PM and start another at 1:00PM. A buffer is needed to debrief the last meeting and to be refreshed and engaged for the next commitment.

Accountability is a type of good stress that elicits focus. Enlist the help of people around you.

Tell a client you'll have a task to them by end of day.

Call a colleague and commit to each other that you are going to do a burst of work for a block of time. Connect at the end of the allocated time to share that you both succeeded.

Or, hire a coach to inspire you.

I offer accountability for my VIP coaching clients.

When clients struggle to stay focused on priority tasks, we take ten minutes to troubleshoot. Set expectations. Then they do the work and confirm it's done by the set deadline.

Many highly successful men and women love this level of accountability. It forces them to ignore the unimportant interruptions.

The good-stress game can change your life.

Choose a priority task or goal, manufacture a deadline, and then add an external accountability source to be sure you deliver.

The prize is restful weekends and memorable vacations – away from work! ▪

COACHING QUESTIONS

What is your most productive time each day? There are likely times when you get your best work done.

What is your least productive time each day? When does your energy dip meaning you're better suited for low intensity tasks or distractions?

In the times when you're in your optimal zone, what's different? Is there a deadline, a goal or accountability?

Play with the idea of a stress scale. It's arbitrary so there is no wrong answer. At what number do you switch from highly productive to overwhelmed or stressed? At what number will you go from in flow to bored? At what number do you best recharge?

What do you notice about your current work schedule? Are there natural high-intensity times versus low-intensity times? What patterns are there now? What's working and what isn't?

TASKS, OBSTACLES AND ADVERSITIES

—

Let's get more specific with part one of the problem-solving framework - Situational Awareness.

Stress has become a catch-all phrase for the never-ending to-do list and the challenges life throws at us.

The truth is: tasks that need to be done and obstacles that need to be solved don't inherently need to be stressful.

It's our emotional and mental connection to tasks and obstacles that turn them into destructive stress.

This stress response occupies more of your capacity than is necessary. It steals much needed space for what's most important in your life.

To ensure this content is relevant to your circumstances, please grab a piece of paper. Spend three minutes writing down everything that is currently causing you stress.

No judgment. No editing. This list is just for you.

It's important to write your stressors down because as you read this chapter, you'll see how this relates to your life. Then you can apply these concepts immediately.

Please do that now. I'll save your spot.

The night before presenting my first keynote on resilience, I decided to do a stress test.

It's a psychological test that measures how much stress you're experiencing from a list of possible challenges.

Each issue is assigned a numerical value indicating how stressful that would be in your life.

For example, losing a loved one could be 48 points. Chronic pain is assigned another number. As are financial troubles, injuries, moves, job changes and other problems. Each is ranked numerically based on the level of stress they cause.

I took the test thinking back to that difficult time in my life that I mentioned earlier.

My stress score was 734.

The legend said, if you have a score over 330, seek professional help immediately.

I don't share this story to be dramatic. I definitely don't want sympathy. In fact, I'm grateful for that time.

It inspired my passion for the topics of resilience and problem-solving. It also forced me to step out of the vortex of stress and learn to love the experience of life.

I share this score because I believe it's an inherently flawed perspective.

Yes, there were a lot of very difficult challenges I faced. But were they stressful?

There are better adjectives. Heartbreaking, exhausting, challenging, painful or all of the above.

Calling everything stress is a cop out.

"Stress" as a blanket term disempowers our ability to cope.

Assigning all issues as stress is a slippery slope. It can contribute to the perspective that you have no control over your "stressful" life.

Maybe what you're living is not a "stressful" life. What if it's just life? What if the ups and downs are normal?

Defaulting anything that isn't perfect to being stressful breeds more stress unnecessarily.

Look at your list of "stressors." Forget the stress word. Instead ask, "Are these tasks, obstacles or adversities?"

Here's the difference.

- A task is something that just has to be done.
- An obstacle is an issue that needs to be solved.
- An adversity is a catastrophic external force that will forever change the way you know your life to be.

The type of issue you're contending with determines the type of solution required.

- Tasks need to be done as efficiently as possible. No drama. No commentary. No emotional allocation required. Just do them. If tasks consistently cause you stress, shifting this can change your life significantly.

- Obstacles need solutions. Most day-to-day obstacles do not require emotional allocation. The more fanfare that surrounds obstacles the harder they are to solve.

- Adversities can't be "solved." They require healing. There is no escaping the grieving process. You need capacity to be able to go through the process. The time needed is often sucked up by tasks and obstacles. Adversities deserve time, reflection, and ultimately acceptance.

Society tends to glorify tasks, "I'm BUSY!" Dramatize obstacles, "OMG, you wouldn't believe it!" And minimize adversity, "I'm FINE." I hope you see how distorted that is.

My hope is for you to flip this. Honour adversities and diminish the emotional intensity applied to tasks and obstacles.

The three types of challenges - tasks, obstacles and adversities - are intertwined.

Too many tasks left undone will cause new obstacles such as missed deadlines or lost clients.

Too many obstacles left unsolved will cause an adversity like a stress-related disease, burnout or company closure.

Adversities will create new obstacles that need to be solved. The solutions to the obstacles will result in tasks which need to be done.

Understanding this relationship between tasks, obstacles and adversities is your ticket to doing all you do without the guilt, destructive stress and risk of burnout. ▪

COACHING QUESTIONS

Write an unfiltered list of all of your challenges.

Have you noticed the tendency for people to bucket every challenge under the word stress? What is your reaction to the word stress?

For the next week, notice every time the word stress is used. Challenge yourself to swap the word with a more accurate description.

Review your list of challenges. Categorize each as a task, obstacle or adversity.

What observations about your stress levels can you make from this exercise?

THE QUEST FOR CONTROL

—

To unpack the tasks, obstacles and adversities concept further, let's discuss control. When high achievers feel control over their life, they are less overwhelmed.

But the quest for control is often misguided. The pandemic added an exclamation mark to that reality!

We don't have control over world events and other peoples' actions. We do, however, have significant control over our stress response to outside circumstances.

Most destructive stress is just a habit that can be broken.

This is important because a lot of time can be wasted on issues beyond our control.

- Complaining a colleague dropped the ball again.
- Resenting that someone else got the promotion.
- Being angry because a competitor made the sale.
- Worrying about the big meeting next week.

All of it is wasted time.

You lose capacity to work and enjoy the present moment when you give copious amounts of energy to issues outside of your control.

For high achievers, feeling out of control can be triggering.

When we face adversity, we have no choice but to go through the roller coaster of emotions. That can make us feel very out-of-control. Well, because we are.

There's no way to avoid the adversity healing process. We must grieve. It sucks. It's heart wrenching. Resisting the worst emotions only prolongs the process.

Adversity is like you're standing on the edge of a sink-hole.

The path once there is no longer available. You must build a bridge to get to the other side. That takes time.

It's why I really want people to stop using the phrase "bounce back" to describe resilience.

The very notion of change is that you can't bounce back. What was there is no longer. It does a disservice to your healing power.

True resilience is not about looking back, it's about being at peace with moving forward.

When you face adversity, your productivity will slip. The brain is foggy. The heart is heavy. That's natural.

The severity of your slippage depends on your resilience and productivity habits that I share in this book.

Thankfully, adversities have a natural honing quality to them. They put priorities into perspective.

When facing adversity, you don't make time for the unimportant.

- Water-cooler gossip seems trivial.
- Distractions are off your radar.
- Saying no to extra work is a no-brainer.
- The should-do list gets an overhaul.

The problem is, after people get through the worst of adversity, they return to old "stressed out" patterns.

There's a PR industry saying, "Let no crisis go to waste." Same in our lives. Be curious about how you focused during adversity and apply those techniques today.

Even though adversity is out of your control, there is hope. You can be grounded and confident (my interpretation of the word control) amidst the worst times. Here's how.

As mentioned earlier, tasks, obstacles and adversities flow into each other. From adversities come new obstacles. The solutions to those obstacles require tasks to implement.

Imagine a control scale going from very high to very low or zero.

We have very low control during adversity.

We have medium-to-high levels of control related to obstacles.

We have a high-to-very-high level of control related to the tasks we must do.

Remember in school they taught us to find the lowest common denominator? Think of that with your challenges.

Tasks are the base of the equation.

I hope that you see how empowering this is.

Take the list you wrote earlier and look at everything causing you stress. Determine which are tasks, obstacles or adversities.

A successful business owner did this exercise during one of my workshops. She was pleasantly surprised. Her list was primarily tasks.

Within a few minutes she realized she was stressed unnecessarily. Tasks do not require the amount of mental and emotional capacity they tend to be given.

If there are adversities on your list, identify the obstacles and sub-obstacles.

Then, use the problem-solving framework to find solutions to the obstacles. That will produce a task list.

For obstacles, the priority is to solve them quickly and effectively. This requires stepping out of the emotion surrounding the obstacle. More about that in the next chapter.

Do tasks as efficiently as possible. That may mean doing them differently. Get curious. Is there a better way?

To make it super simple:

Adversities -----> heal.
Obstacles -----> solve.
Tasks -----> do.

An example of the difference between tasks, obstacles and adversities is a drop in revenue for a business.

If the business is operational, there is no adversity, even though it may feel like it. Low revenue is an obstacle.

Using the problem-solving framework, create a game plan to get new sales.

The tasks could be to call prospects, tweak marketing materials or ask current clients for referrals.

A personal example is my surgery that resulted in nerve pain and other physical complications.

Before I understood resilience, I was desperate to go back to my pre-surgery body. My goal was to "bounce back."

I remember crying to my doctor for an hour. I begged him to fix me. His answer was for me to re-evaluate my expectations for my life and consider going on disability.

That was an adversity. I needed to grieve my life pre-pain.

I left the hospital determined to be resilient. I wrote down all the obstacles that came from my pain.

One obstacle was that driving myself long distances on the highway was very painful. Most of my clients were a 2.5 hour drive away, but it was unsafe.

I looked at the obstacle strategically, rather than emotionally. I brainstormed ideas for a chauffeur.

A professional driver wasn't in my budget. Thankfully, my Mom was willing to help. She drove me safely back and forth to my keynotes and workshops.

I slept; she drove. It worked.

Adversity — surgery repercussions.
Obstacle — couldn't drive myself safely to my speeches.
Task — call Mom to ask for help.

If I kept spending my time trying to "fix" the surgery outcomes, I would never be where I am today—working full-time with a successful business and handling my physical pain medication free.

Whenever you are stressed or you face tough times, ask,

"Is this a task, an obstacle or an adversity?" Once you know that, you'll know the next steps to take.

Do tasks more efficiently and solve obstacles faster. That will free capacity to heal from adversities.

It also means that you will condense the time it takes to complete tasks and solve problems.

Yielding greater outputs from each hour during the week makes it easy to Take Back Your Weekends. ▪

COACHING QUESTIONS

What does having a sense of control mean to you?

In what ways, if any, is feeling a sense of control important to you?

Looking at your list of challenges, what about each issue is within your control?

For the next week, observe your relationship to control. How often do you allocate mental and emotional resources to issues outside your control?

For each obstacle and adversity on your list, find the root tasks that need to be done. How can this empower you to free capacity to heal or solve?

SELF–AWARENESS
—

Self-Awareness is critical if you want to change patterns and solve problems faster.

It doesn't mean you'll automatically find the solution, but without self-awareness, it's hard to find solutions that stick.

The risk with Self-Awareness is it can easily switch to self judgment and self criticism. These are extra obstacles that waste mental and emotional capacity.

Instead, I encourage you to approach Self-Awareness through a lens of compassionate curiosity.

I have recovered from being VERY self-critical. The way I stopped the habit was to adopt this philosophy of compassionate curiosity.

When I did something that would typically cause embarrassment, self-criticism or harsh judgment, I flipped the script.

Hmm that's interesting, I wonder why I did it that way? Is MUCH kinder than: *You're such an idiot. How could you?*

Curiosity allowed me to accept that I did what I did with the knowledge I had then. Now, thanks to that experience, I have a new perspective to choose differently next time.

If you've heard me speak, you know I'm not shy. I proudly share examples from my life that taught me these lessons.

If it weren't for those mistakes and tough times, my resilience and problem-solving message would not be impacting thousands today and hopefully one day millions!

I still repeat the same mistakes and have to remind myself to take my own advice. I still turn ice cubes into snowmen (You'll discover what that means in the next chapter.)

Instead of beating myself up for being human, I embrace the ups and downs of personal and professional growth. It's not a straight line.

My philosophy is "grateful now and aiming higher."

Self-awareness mixed with grace for yourself and a commitment to continual personal growth is powerful. ▪

COACHING QUESTIONS

Do you harshly criticize yourself? In what ways?

How does switching from self judgment to compassionate curiosity feel for you?

Write a story about a time when you were very self critical. Now, rewrite the story from a perspective of empathy, compassion and curiosity. How does the story change?

In what ways could you be kinder to yourself?

Are there circumstances that you're currently judging that would be better served by allowing yourself some grace?

THE ICE CUBE THAT BECAME A SNOWMAN

—

Imagine every task you have to complete as an ice cube. Imagine every obstacle to be solved as a bit larger cube.

Your job is to melt those ice cubes as efficiently and effectively as you can.

The sooner you melt your ice cubes, the more time you have left for what matters most to you. Family, friends, self-care, creative pursuits. Whatever you want.

Because you're talented, melting ice cubes is easy.

But we don't just melt the ice cubes, do we? No, we also have access to a mound of snow at all times.

The snow represents:

1. Misplaced emotions
2. Negative story lines
3. Barriers to performance i.e., worry, judgment, not setting boundaries and frequent interruptions

As part of the human experience, we tend to dunk our ice cubes into the snow. That makes them harder to melt.

As each layer of snow is packed around the ice cube it grows into a snowball, then a boulder, then you've got a full snowman to melt.

What's easier to melt? An ice cube or a snowman?

To Take Back Your Weekends – blast through the snow!

Let's examine this snow a bit more to truly understand how the snowman metaphor relates to stolen capacity.

The first layer of snow that gets packed on the ice cube is misplaced emotions. It can show itself in unexpected ways.

For example, the angry customer who takes out his life frustration on the innocent cashier.

The person who feels miserable, unfulfilled and unseen then aggressively targets users online.

The colleague who is irritable with you because of a big fight with a loved one before coming to work.

Maybe you find yourself snapping at someone when they innocently ask a question. Really, you're hurt by a snide comment a peer made or you're scared about cash flow.

Anytime emotion is misdirected to the wrong subject – that's another layer of snow.

Intense emotions can overshadow issues that don't deserve negativity. That's when we need to stop and become self-aware. Get curious about the real issue.

Negative story lines are the next layer of snow. This includes harsh self-talk as well as what you speak aloud to others and about them.

- *I'll never get this done.*
- *OMG, I'm SO BUSY!*
- *I hate doing this task.*
- *These reports are useless. No one will ever read them.*

These seem like innocent one-liners. They aren't. They add extra snow to the tasks at hand. Moaning and complaining steal capacity from the workday.

I don't believe in pretending it's all sunshine and rainbows. There's no need to say, "I love doing taxes" when clearly, no one loves doing taxes, except maybe accountants.

Just do the taxes. No negative commentary required.

The attitude attached to a task influences the efficiencies with which it can be done. Eliminate the fanfare from every task. You'll be shocked by the extra capacity you discover.

It's easy to underestimate how much work capacity is sucked away by throwaway one-liners, non-constructive conversations and gloomy news cycles.

Another way negative story lines turn into snow packed around ice cubes is by the messages you absorb from what you read and hear.

A client found himself getting angrier and more irritable during COVID. When we did some digging, he realized he had the 24-hour news channel on 24 hours a day.

It's tough to be in a good mood with constant negativity as your primary input. Be informed, but limit consumption.

I had lunch with a friend. She's an executive at a national company. Three weeks earlier head office had sent her a directive for a new report to be completed.

"I'm so angry. Head office is clueless. I think it's time to look for a new job."

I listened. Wow this must be serious. How long will this new report take?

She leaned back and laughed. *"Fifteen minutes."*

The truth was, she felt unsupported by the company.

Her Task Circle was spinning out of control. She needed to off-load work she'd absorbed when a colleague quit. No one was listening to her. She needed to feel validated.

She took her frustrations out on a report. It was three weeks overdue but could have been done in minutes with a small amount of focus.

Not doing the small task led to three weeks of annoyance, anger and dropping the ball. All that frustration because of misplaced emotions and negative story lines. Those wasted hours were better spent enjoying downtime.

Do a quick check when you're stressed. Get a sense of any snow that's piling up around the ice cube.

Ask yourself, am I emotional about something legitimate and redirecting it to another, unrelated issue?

Now you've got an ice cube (the task or obstacle) that's turned into a snowball thanks to some misplaced emotion.

If negative words or story lines are added the snowball grows bigger into another section of the snowman.

Use self-awareness routinely to consider the words and story lines being used to interpret the issue. Do they have a negative slant?

If you also believe that stress is generated by perspective, then all story lines that go beyond the real issue are technically fiction. Why not choose a positive point of view?

The third layer of snow is represented by barriers to performance. Add these to the mix and you've got a full snowman.

Remember, the task or obstacle is still JUST an ice cube.

Barriers to performance are any habits that take you away from your sweet spot of performance, productivity and profitability. Consider them anything that unnecessarily makes a task harder to do or an obstacle more complicated to solve.

Some examples are:
- Worry
- Procrastination
- Glorifying busy
- Blame
- Judgment
- Gossip
- Constant complaints
- Perfectionism
- Inability to say no
- Ineffective time management
- Lack of focus
- Change resistance
- Drama

- Catastrophizing
- Closed-minded thinking
- Stubbornness
- Micromanaging
- Pessimism
- Past-focused
- Defensiveness
- Territorial marking
- Constant lateness
- Comparison
- Resentment
- Lack of prioritization
- Frequent interruptions
- Poor planning
- Victim mentality
- Unclear boundaries
- Meeting-heavy schedule
- Unrealistic expectations of yourself and others

We've all experienced some, or all, of these to varying degrees at different points in our life.

For example, it's impossible to find a person who has never worried or procrastinated.

I know I used to waste hours worrying and procrastinating.

These limiting habits are a natural part of life. The game is to minimize their negative impact on your day-to-day.

For example, if you worry for three days before a meeting, apply the problem-solving framework and cut that to ten minutes.

During my speech, a leader realized how frustrated she was by a disorganized office. She decided it was just an ice cube to melt, but she had made it into a snowman by procrastinating.

It only took her a few hours to get everything sorted. Her peace-of-mind moving forward was so much better. She lost that nagging feeling that plagued her.

How much faster and more effective would you be during the week if you stopped procrastinating and got organized? Multiply that impact by every barrier to performance that applies to you.

Please don't get overwhelmed by how long the list is. The process is to pick ONE. Apply the problem-solving framework. Minimize its impact. Then pick another. That's how you Take Back Your Weekends! ▪

COACHING QUESTIONS

What's your initial reaction to the concept of The Ice Cube That Became The Snowman?

For the next week, get really curious and notice "ice cubes" and any "snow" that may be making tasks and obstacles harder than they need to be.

When you feel stressed, anxious or overwhelmed, jot down the words you're using and the story lines you're crafting.

With this clarity, can you choose different words and alternative, more positive story lines?

Considering your inputs, what's the most negative influence? Your inner voice, conversations with others, or what you read or watch?

Given mood can be greatly influenced by what we think, hear and say, what percentage of your inputs are positive versus negative?

SOLUTION ACTIVATION

—

When finding a solution, there are principles that can guide you to the best decision.

These principles contribute to the way of thinking that makes it easier to solve problems and do tasks. This ultimately frees your capacity to heal from adversities and enjoy time for what matters most to you.

You'll notice this chapter isn't full of techniques to deal with each of the barriers to performance. While I've shared potential solutions throughout the book, telling you how to deal with each would do you a disservice.

Every solution is different. The best way for one person to succeed is not the same way for another.

The best solutions for each person are uncovered via situational awareness and self-awareness. There are too many variables.

My goal is to teach you a better way to de-construct problems. Then, use your brilliance to find the best solution in any given circumstance.

I know you can get results because you've been solving problems your whole life. Add what I've shared to your current talents. There is no obstacle you can't solve.

As a quick recap, some of the foundational concepts are:

- The difference between good and destructive stress
- My problem-solving framework
- Tasks, obstacles and adversities
- The scale of control
- Self-awareness through compassionate curiosity
- The Ice Cube That Became The Snowman
- The Task Circle Method (more on that soon)

Incorporating each of the above into your day-to-day life will remove unnecessarily stress.

Adopting a new way of thinking and interrupting patterns is a journey.

You don't decide to never complain again and poof, you only see rainbows for the rest of your life. Personal growth is not a linear experience.

Remind yourself of that. Embrace the ups and downs. Dips don't mean you're failing – they mean you're growing.

As you embark on your personal and professional journey, here are five principles of Solution Activation to guide you.

You may find that one or two of these resonates most for you. That's great. Focus on them. These principles are meant to help you ride the waves of being resilient.

Less Snow = Better Solutions

I hope that the Ice Cube That Became the Snowman metaphor makes this obvious. Whenever I am struggling to process something, I de-construct the situation to determine the ice cube and any snow that may be clouding my perspective.

Your Second Response Is the Priority – Get To It ASAP

You've spent decades reinforcing patterns. That means the same habit is likely to be repeated. It won't change without a concerted effort.

The first, less desirable response will happen by default. The goal is to shorten the length and intensity of that reaction. The sooner you can choose differently, the better.

Eventually the hope is to catch yourself mid-stream. Then switch your response in real-time.

That's why I'm so passionate about self-awareness.

The more self-aware you are of your reaction in the moment, the sooner you can interrupt a pattern and choose a different response.

- Notice you're being unkind? Choose to spread kindness instead. Change your tone mid-sentence.

- Notice you're worrying about a meeting next week? Go through the problem-solving framework to gain perspective. Every time the worry thought re-emerges, practice mental discipline to flip the script and trust your future self.

- Have you said yes when you wish you said no? Call the person and change your answer.

As you practice new behaviours, your first response will slowly disappear and new habits will emerge by default.

A Slip Does Not Mean You Need to Stop

Further to the last principle, you will fail along the way. That's part of the human experience of growth. There is no finish line when your goal is to become the best version of yourself. The goal post keeps moving as you evolve.

It's like dieting. I remember when I used to diet a lot. I'd binge on Friday night, and then Saturday think, *Oh, what's the point? I'm already off track. I may as well eat this, too.*

No! A slip to an old pattern is not an excuse to give up on the goal! You can choose to get back on track.

Look For The Next Best Step And Take It

It's easy to want to know how an entire solution will unfold. I haven't found anyone yet who can accurately predict the future. Wanting to know the entire solution can stop progress and keep you from taking the necessary steps.

There are often too many variables to be able to design a full solution from the starting gate.

When it comes to personal growth – take the next best step. Evaluate its effectiveness. Then, take the next best step after that, which may be to tweak the first step.

Continually walk along the path until you reach your desired outcome.

Trust Yourself

There is no crystal ball. There is no magic wand to make your problems disappear. While that may sound depressing, the truth is, I see it as empowering.

You've made it this far. Yes, you've faced challenges. Yes, you're human and have made mistakes. Yes, you have patterns you aim to change.

AND you're still reading!

That says to me that you're committed to continual personal and professional improvement.

You've got everything it takes to be successful at the level you desire. The only thing in your way is not trusting yourself to step fully into your brilliance. It's time. ▪

COACHING QUESTIONS

Of the seven foundational concepts I've shared so far, what's resonated the most for you? Why?

Of the five principles of solution activation, which resonates the most with you? Why?

Is there any "snow" that is making your life harder unnecessarily?

Pick one principle of solution activation and brainstorm ideas on how you can integrate that into your decision-making and problem-solving.

Thinking of Solution Activation Principles, what could you do differently the next time you face an obstacle?

APPLYING MY PROBLEM-SOLVING FRAMEWORK

—

Pick one issue and apply the framework. Let's use an example of a popular barrier — constant interruptions.

Leaders blame interruptions for why they don't get work done during regular hours. They find no one disturbs them on the weekend, late at night or early in the morning, so it's easier to be productive.

The truth is interruptions won't stop on their own. To Take Back Your Weekends you're going to need to tweak your approach and set boundaries.

Leaders justify the lack of boundaries related to interruptions. *My team needs me. I don't want to seem unapproachable or rude. We have an open-door policy.*

Open-door policy is fine. Door-mat policy is not okay.

Let's use my problem-solving framework to fix the time-suck of frequent interruptions.

You can use the problem-solving framework on any barrier to performance or other challenge. All it takes is an understanding of the basic frameworks I've already shared, plus some curiosity, creativity and a pen and paper.

Remember there are three parts: Situational Awareness, Self-Awareness and Solution Activation.

Situational Awareness:

To implement Situational Awareness, answer three questions.

1. What's the real issue? (a.k.a. The ice cube)
2. Is this a task, an obstacle or an adversity?
3. What about this is within or out of my control?

One client spent years caught in the stress vortex. He was busy, but not consistently productive. Despite his outward success, he was under living his potential and frustrated.

I challenged him to track his activities for one week.

He called me at the end of day ONE. "Allison, you're absolutely right. It's so obvious what's sucking my time. I had no idea. Now I believe I can fix this."

I challenge you. Get a clear picture of the tasks you do, how long they take, the conversations you have and the distractions you encounter. Take an inventory.

This list requires zero judgment. Please don't edit the items. It's important to see where you're losing time on unimportant tasks.

Based on a daily inventory of your tasks, you may find you get interrupted, on average, ten times per day. (I know, if only the number were that low!)

If each stoppage lasts two minutes, that's 20 minutes a day away from your priority tasks.

Next, you have to account for the time it takes you to refocus on what you were doing. That's at least another two minutes (minimum.)

That's 40 minutes a day, stolen because of interruptions.

Some leaders tell me that interruptions take about ten minutes each, not two. Multiply 10 by 10 minutes.

Now you're facing a lost-productivity problem of 100 minutes/day.

There are varying statistics on how long it takes to return to flow. Let's say it's half the time you're interrupted. So, five minutes. That's another 50 minutes taken from your sweet spot of performance, productivity and profitability.

I get it. Interruptions are often part of your leadership role. Helping team members. Taking phone calls. Putting out fires. All reasonable.

BUT to Take Back Your Weekends, you've got to fulfil your leadership duties AND solve the problem that is sucking between 40 minutes and two hours from each work day.

What if every person in your company has the same problem of dealing with constant interruptions?

For those working from home, these may be low estimates.

Even if you solved half of the problem, that jump in productivity, compounded daily, is the ticket to Take Back Your Weekends.

Imagine this. Interruptions only account for one barrier to performance. I've listed 31 above.

Can you see how it's absolutely possible to take control of your time by blasting through the snow?

Ask yourself if the issue of "frequent interruptions" is a task, an obstacle or an adversity?

This can be determined by two ways. First ask, "Is this something I need to do, solve or heal?" Second, determine your level of control related to the situation.

Since it's an issue that needs to be solved and you can control your boundaries related to interruptions, we can conclude that it's an obstacle.

While you can't control other people's behaviours, you can minimize interruptions by your actions.

Some initial ideas:

- The boundaries you set
- The empowerment of your team to problem-solve first instead of defaulting to ask you the question
- Carving focused time blocks
- The notifications you have dinging around you

Now it's your turn. What would you add to the list? Brainstorm aspects of the situation that you can control or meaningfully influence. Consider what's out of your control.

Interrupt unhealthy patterns and minimize barriers to performance by focusing on aspects within your control.

The items you put on your "what I can control list" will be your key to empowerment.

That's Situational Awareness in action.

All of that thinking took me a couple of minutes. Typing it took longer.

This is a fast exercise. If the framework becomes cumbersome, it will cause a new obstacle.

Self-Awareness:

Now the fun begins. You'll need to get really curious about your reaction to interruptions and how your actions may be making them worse or enabling them.

Use your creativity to ask yourself questions from every angle of self-awareness. Consider all three responses - emotional, mental and physical.

Remember earlier I said that self-awareness is a rabbit hole. It really is. Get super curious about every aspect of your interruptions pattern – without judgment! When you find an answer that's good enough, stop searching.

If we were coaching together here are some questions I might ask:
- How do you differentiate high priority interruptions versus wasted time?
- Are you spending too long at your desk and welcome the distraction?
- Is it easier to answer questions than do your own work?

- Have you created an environment where your team doesn't troubleshoot on their own?
- Are you an obliger meaning you feel fulfilled by helping others, even if it means dropping your priorities?
- Are you physically positioning yourself to encourage more frequent interruptions?

This could seem like a lot of digging for an issue you're already navigating. After all, you're successful despite the interruptions, right?

Imagine time is money and every hour was worth $10,000. If you were draining ten thousand dollars a day, you'd invest the time to stop the leak. Your time is priceless. Isn't the effort worth it to Take Back Your Weekends?

Invest in finding these answers for yourself and to empower your team to follow your lead.

Imagine your productivity boost when you identify and minimize a ten-hour time suck each week.

Could you skip working on the weekends when you do that?

Absolutely.

Solution Activation:

Now that you're clear on what's happening and how you're reacting to it, keep those factors in mind as you brainstorm solutions. You can do this with another person.

I can think of ten ideas off the top of my head. So can you. It's not hard. Allow ideas to flow without prejudging.

To accentuate why Self-Awareness is critical before moving to Solution Activation, let's play with this a bit.

One way you could brainstorm to minimize interruptions is to close your door. Would-be interrupters see the closed door and keep walking because you're unavailable.

You nod your head and say, "Yes, closing my door is a good idea. I'll do that."

Yet, despite agreement that it's a good idea, a week later your door is open again and interruptions are rampant.

Through self-awareness we would have uncovered that closing your door would never work for you.

Through self-awareness, we may have uncovered how important the interruptions are to you. Perhaps that's the only way you get a break.

A closed door means there's no relief from your workload, which is unsustainable. Perhaps the solution you're really looking for is how to proactively take breaks. That's a different ice cube.

Perhaps you value accessibility. A closed door makes you feel uncomfortable because you feel isolated from others.

In this example the obvious answer – a closed door – is not the solution that will stick. You need the right fix for you.

Perhaps there's another way to indicate that you're in focused mode and don't want to be interrupted. A special wave, an "I'm focused" hat you wear or a sign on the door.

In my office building there are hundreds of co-tenants. It's an interruption waiting to happen. Especially given the big glass window to my private office.

As a community there are guidelines to minimize unwanted interruptions. Two tactics were adopted.

1. If you're wearing a headset in the common areas and have both ear buds in, that means you're focused. If you wear one, it means you're open to interruptions.
2. If an office door is closed, that means you're in focused mode. Only interrupt if it's absolutely essential. If it's ajar, there's focus wiggle room.

I added a third option. Through self-awareness I realized that I felt "bad" with a closed door. Through the window I saw them, they saw me, but I ignored them. It felt rude.

I created two signs to tape on my office window. One said, "Focused work in progress, please help me stay on track."

The other said, "ON AIR! Please visit later." Obviously the second sign was posted when I was on the radio or recording a podcast.

Over the years as a tenant in the building, I rarely felt the interruptions were significant. It's because of the tactics.

Without them, there would have been dozens of potential interruptions a day. Especially for me. Squirrel.

Once you've brainstormed potential solutions, pick one idea. Test it. See if it works. Tweak it.

A week later, stack the next best idea on top of the first. Tweak that one until your issue of constant interruptions is no longer a time suck.

You've likely had decades of reinforcing the barrier to performance. It's going to be the consistent small tweaks, that over time, will get the biggest results.

Let the principles of Solution Activation guide you on this journey. When you find yourself slipping into old habits, that's okay. Get back on track as fast as possible.

Start with one barrier to performance. Then another and another. After a year, your life will be very different.

An executive heard me speak on a podcast. I talked about how worrying is a down payment on a problem you may never have. How the habit of worrying can literally steal hours from your happiness.

The message resonated.

He'd spent his whole Christmas holiday stressing about the upcoming tax season. It distracted him from his family.

He worried if he had enough staff. Worried about office dynamics. Worried about his clients. He just worried a lot.

Worry was his habit. Despite his professional success, it was stealing joy and hours from his life.

That's how we started our coaching relationship. A year later, I asked how his Christmas holidays went. He said, "Fantastic. I didn't worry about work once!"

He was committed to shifting his barrier to optimal performance. He not only took back his weekends, but he also took back his vacations. You can too! ▪

COACHING QUESTIONS

Review the list of barriers to performance on Pages 86 & 87. Which are your top three time thieves?

Pick one. How is it negatively impacting your happiness or productivity? List some examples.

Apply my problem-solving framework. What's the real issue?

What's within your control?

What about this is a task, obstacle or adversity? Determine if this is a "do," "solve" or "heal" issue.

How are you reacting mentally, emotionally and physically?

Are you complicating the issue unnecessarily?

Brainstorm three to five possible solutions. Which will you do first? What will success look like?

MANAGING THE TASKS

—

The problem-solving framework helps you blast through the snow, but what do you do with all the ice cubes that are left?

Once you eliminate the misplaced emotions, negative story lines and barriers to performance, there's still lots of work to be done.

As mentioned earlier, I've tried many productivity systems. This is the approach that works the best in my experience.

All you need is pen and paper.

If you love using software to track your tasks – go for it. This method will work either way.

If you use software, be sure it's not complicating matters.

Personally, I like paper because it's fast. I just scribble items in my Task Circle and forget them, freeing mental capacity.

Plus, I love the satisfaction of putting a red check mark beside completed tasks. Each day I can see the culmination of my efforts.

Small wins equal big motivation.

Before I share my Task Circle Method with you, let's explore four popular task-tracking concepts that are not exceptionally effective and why.

1. The traditional to-do list that includes a long list of tasks.

You'd think this would be effective. After all, everything is in one place. The problem is there is very little rhyme or reason to the list. It's just long and overwhelming.

It's hard to tell the fast from the long tasks. Priorities are listed with non-priorities. For those who wear many hats, there is no obvious separation for what goes with what.

2. Mixing your tasks with your meeting notes.

Some professionals have one notebook that they use for every meeting. They diligently write notes and are careful to write their tasks as they go.

While this approach looks organized, it can backfire.

I did this for years. In fact, my twenties and early thirties were spent with my lists and notes mixed into a notebook. I spent a lot of time flipping through pages.

Often I missed tasks. It felt overwhelming because the tasks were alongside the notes. Sifting through all those details to find exactly what to do next took extra mental capacity.

The content that supports doing the tasks needs to be separate from the tasks themselves. Transfer tasks from meeting notes to your master Task Circle.

3. Batched by project status.

Most systems default to a version of "to do", "doing" and "done." It's a fancier version of the long to-do list. This does very little to minimize overwhelm.

It doesn't account for priorities, length of time for tasks or the various hats of responsibility you wear.

Listing what's in progress is not as helpful as seeing what needs to be done now.

Scrolling through long lists of tasks can plummet your output per hour. To Take Back Your Weekends, it's critical to find time sucks - hidden or obvious.

4. Batched by activity type.

This is when someone collects all like tasks together. Items like phone calls, emails, writing proposals, meetings, and creative time would be grouped together.

Then, when you sit down to make phone calls, you'd make all calls at once. Logically this makes sense. With the phone already in your hand, why not keep dialling?

The catch with batching by activity type is that it doesn't account for what happens if a client needs a report, an email, a phone call and some creative work completed.

Do you wait and do each task at a different time?

It's just not practical.

There are only two activities I recommend batching. One is errands outside of the home or office. The second is money matters such as invoicing and paying bills. Emails can be batched, too. Ask me how on social media.

Many coaching clients have said they've tried bucketing, but it doesn't work.

That is because they are bucketing by the wrong variable.

These frustrations with typical systems are why I have created the Task Circle Method.

The name is intended to be a reminder that the list does not end. Feeling emotionally charged by that reality is wasted energy.

Remember, tasks are just a bunch of ice cubes that need to be melted as efficiently and effectively as possible.

How you choose to organize your Task Circle is critical to your productivity. It's how you'll Take Back Your Weekends. ▪

COACHING QUESTIONS

How are you currently tracking your tasks?

What about your current tracking system works well?

What about your current system is not effective?

Do you feel organized when you start to work? If not, how much time do you believe you lose each day to disorganization?

Are you open to trying a different task-tracking system?

CREATING YOUR TASK CIRCLE

—

Before you start, do a brain dump of all the current tasks to be done.

This will help you identify themes and allow you to input data into your first Task Circle.

Output per hour shrinks when you constantly switch between areas of responsibility.

The point of the Task Circle is to prioritize focused work blocks based on each area of responsibility rather than the individual tasks.

You can't wear more than one hat at once.

I used to jump all over the place. One minute I'd make sales calls, the next I'd write a Linked In post and the next I'd send an invoice.

It was scattered and my productivity paid for it.

Instead of jumping from one bucket to another, streamline your thinking to wear one hat at a time.

Choose one hat. Wear it for a focused stint. Take It off.

Have a break and then choose which hat to wear next. You may have to wear the same hat multiple times in one day as you work through the priorities in the bucket.

Within each focused work block, leverage good stress by incorporating a goal, a deadline and accountability.

Output per hour will sky-rocket!

Here are the steps to create a Task Circle:
1. Choose your areas of responsiblity for your buckets
2. List tasks related to each bucket's theme
3. Estimate how long each task will take
4. Split larger tasks into smaller tasks
5. Prioritize tasks within each bucket
6. Prioritize your schedule by area of responsibility
7. Focus, repeat and tweak as required

Once you understand each step, it only takes a few minutes each week to get organized.

Choose Your Areas of Responsibility

The biggest challenge with managing workload is the number of hats worn by many professionals.

For example, in my world as a solo businessperson, aside from a few virtual contractors, I "do it all." That means I wear many hats throughout the day.

One minute I'm the sales person, the next I'm preparing for a client speech and the next I'm contemplating a PR strategy. My brain has many reasons to shift gears a lot.

The buckets of responsibility in my Task Circle are:

- Clients
- Sales
- Marketing
- Admin
- Personal
- Project (I generally have one or two projects - like this book - that would overcrowd another area. A big project gets its own bucket until it's complete.)

Reflect on your areas of responsibility. Look for themes from your full to-do list and your job description. This will give you an idea on what to name your buckets.

Clients have had different categories such as:

- Investor Relations
- Human Resources
- Media/PR (which I include under marketing)
- Research
- Team Development
- Executive Relations
- Reports
- Volunteer Activities
- Parent/Partner/House Manager (You could have a separate Task Circle for personal activities.)

The idea is to take that great big, long to-do list that has no context and separate it into the different hats you wear.

Perhaps you don't have that many hats. It's just client service tasks all day. No problem.

A friend says marketing and admin slip because her clients consume her time. The list of tasks is very long.

To minimize her overwhelm and integrate her missing areas, I suggest categorizing based on service offerings. She has four types of clients: Publishing, Coaching, Media Relations and Training.

There are her first four buckets. Marketing and Admin round out her Task Circle.

That's more manageable than having 15 clients on a long list, each with ten subtasks due this week.

Create your circle in whatever way that makes sense.

If you have more than six or seven buckets (five is ideal), then either your buckets are too specific or you legitimately have too many responsibilities. It's time to shift your ways.

Hire someone, outsource work, or start saying no. You can't do it all. To Take Back Your Weekends, choices are required.

For example, I used to have a Volunteer bucket. Most days I had more tasks in that bucket than any other.

This system helped me realize how lopsided my activities were. I spent more time volunteering than I did selling, marketing my services and serving my clients.

While I love giving to charities and causes, my health, my family and my business are my priorities.

My pace of giving wasn't sustainable. Something had to give. (Pun intended.)

Now, when I have a volunteer commitment, it goes into my personal bucket. When that overflows, I know I've taken on too many volunteer commitments.

There are many insights that can be gleaned from this process. For example, if you're a small business owner, you may find that you have so much client work that you neglect marketing efforts.

Marketing today secures clients tomorrow. Without consistent effort, eventually projects end and revenue dips.

As a leader responsible for a team, you may notice that your Human Resources bucket is overflowing with tasks to support and lead your team.

You could explore options to better empower your team to achieve success without your continual input.

Perhaps it's time to engage an HR specialist for a part-time contract or mentor another leader to take the reigns.

When I neglect the admin bucket (I find it's the easiest to push) it'll start overflowing with small tasks. Ironically, it's usually the fastest bucket to clear.

The Task Circle could show that you rarely prioritize your personal commitments. No wonder you never get a break or spend time with friends.

That's when you turn to the intersection of goals, deadlines and accountability to be sure your personal bucket - or any neglected bucket - gets integrated into your life.

As I begin to share these steps, I've taken a picture of how my Task Circle starts.

Take the concept and make it your own.

Use technology. Write bigger. Write smaller. Put each bucket on it's own paper. Use a notebook. Use software. Draw pretty pictures. Do what works for you.

The point is to have an absolutely clear expectation of what to do when you choose to wear each hat and the order in which the tasks need to be done.

I start my Task Circle with my bucket headings:

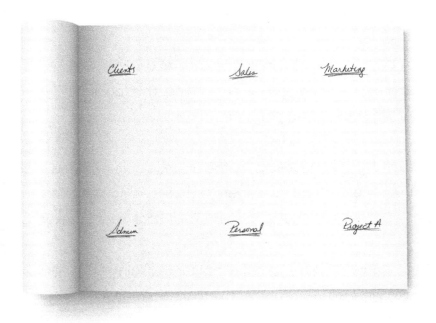

List Tasks Related To Each Bucket's Theme

The Task Circle gathers tasks related to the same areas of responsibility. The idea is that when you choose to wear a hat, you ONLY focus on tasks related to that role.

If you're in HR mode, ignore tasks related to client delivery and vice versa. It takes mental discipline to hone in on one bucket at a time.

Look at your to-do list in chunks, not as a whole. Smaller task groupings are less overwhelming. This focus will improve your output per hour.

Remember, we're looking for the nuance of finding ten minutes here, 30 minutes there and three minutes over here. Collectively, that's how you Take Back Your Weekends.

For your first Task Circle, take that large brain dump I asked you to write earlier. Transfer the tasks from your master list into the appropriate bucket.

A task could be "quarterly report." That would get placed under your Investor Relations bucket heading.

Another task could be "review long term care homes for my aunt." That would go under the Personal category.

A task to "create a Linked In strategy" would be included in the marketing bucket.

Keep going until your entire to-do list is placed into the proper categories.

If a task doesn't fit just pick a bucket that makes sense.

If that happens consistently, add a new category.

For example, a client who is an advisor has to stay current on the news, market trends and compliance issues. Her buckets didn't account for this role. She created a new bucket called "Research" to ensure it was prioritized.

When you sit for a work block, focus on one category at a time. Ignore anything that doesn't directly relate to the hat you're wearing.

My Task Circle ends up looking like six mini lists under each of the headings shown above.

Estimate How Long Each Task Will Take

Go through your Task Circle and estimate how long each task will take. This helps you plot what to do in a work block.

When you start your focused stint, you can choose. Do you want to do the super fast, easy tasks to gain momentum? Or, do you want to start with the harder tasks first to feel accomplished?

There is no wrong way. It's about finding the process that works best for you.

Doing the time estimate gives you a sense of how long tasks actually take. Sometimes you may overestimate or underestimate. It doesn't matter.

It's all data that helps you plan for next time. It also helps you understand where your time goes.

When you have a small gap of time, you can easily turn to your Task Circle and see a fast task and complete it.

I've noticed when I estimate how long something will take to do, it gives me a hit of inspiration. I'll think, it's only 15 minutes, why not just get it done?

Another important reason to get a sense of how long a task will take is that it will show you if you're putting too much or too little time into tasks.

If an activity feels draining, have a conversation with a colleague. Ask if it takes them the same amount of time. Get curious if there's a faster, more effective way to melt the ice cube.

Split Larger Tasks Into Smaller Tasks

One way to get overwhelmed is to put large tasks on your list. Most big projects are a series of smaller, fast tasks.

Ideally, every task that's on your list would take fewer than 15 minutes.

Here's why.

If a task takes two hours, you know you need to carve a lot of time in your calendar to get it done.

You may avoid starting it because you don't have a two-hour window. Worse, you may save it for Saturday morning because that's when you'll have a full work block available.

Instead, break the big projects down into smaller fast tasks that collectively will result in the larger task getting done.

When I hosted a podcast, it was a lot of work. I noticed that I would put it in my Task Circle and then avoid it.

"Podcast" as a task was overwhelming.

It was too big to find the time.

Then I switched tactics. I wrote podcast, but then added sub tasks:
- Choose topic
- Map content
- Record session
- Edit recording

- Create artwork
- Write description
- Upload for distribution
- Share on social

Each of these items were manageable. If I had a ten minute window, I could choose to do a smaller task.

When I used a full work block to produce the podcast, I had a road map of exactly how to get it done. There was no wasting time trying to figure out what to do next.

This approach also helped me stop procrastination. The workload seemed less overwhelming.

Checking off each smaller task gave me momentum. It also meant if I didn't get the full podcast produced, I knew exactly where I was in the process for later.

Prioritize Tasks Within Each Bucket

All of the tasks related to an area of responsibility will be collected in each bucket. When you choose to focus on a role, you just have to look to that bucket's list.

Within each bucket, there needs to be a level of prioritization. I use the alphabet to make it obvious.

This takes the guess work out of what to do next. You just go to A, then when it's done, do B, then C, then D and so on.

When the time block is done, you can decide if you achieved enough to remove that hat for the day or if you need another focused work block to keep going.

Remember, the reason this is called a Task Circle is to remind you that the list will never end.

While it's fun to put a red check mark beside every task within a bucket, it rarely happens. I generally start a new Task Circle on a fresh piece of paper before the tasks within each bucket are complete.

Even if you get it all done, the bucket will be filled again! Embrace that! It's a good thing. If all the buckets were empty, you'd have nothing left to do.

Prioritize Your Schedule By Area Of Responsibility

Prioritising time by area of responsibility allows you to get in flow using one part of your brain.

Block time for each bucket based on your energy, your priorities and the amount of time you have available.

A factor that's critical to your output per hour is understanding your natural energy flow.

What time of day are you most productive or creative? When does your focus dip?

For example, I do my best writing first thing in the morning.

When I have an active project like writing this book, I block bursts of focused writing time accordingly.

It would not make sense to use my prime energy time to wear my admin hat. That's saved for when my brain is in low gear.

It's helpful to have a sense of how you will prioritize your buckets.

For me, my general order is Clients, Sales, Marketing, Projects, Personal and Admin.

This prioritization is just a guide. Professionals with lots on the go need to embrace that priorities fluctuate.

For example, just because Admin is last in terms of an overarching priority on how I allocate my time, it can't be ignored forever.

Personal is toward the end because most of those tasks don't require my prime brain power. Tasks that make money and are integral to my company's success, go first.

If you only ever prioritize clients then everything else will get pushed. Most likely you'll have to do it on the weekends.

There are many reasons that will influence which category takes precedence on any given day or within a work block.

It could be your meeting schedule, external deadlines, your energy or life circumstances that cause you to shift gears.

Look at your week view on your calendar. Where are the gaps of at least 45 to 75 minutes?

Plug in your focused time blocks and which hat you will wear for that time.

The popular "Pomodoro Method" suggests you work in 25 minute intervals. I find I can't get enough momentum to make that approach worthwhile.

My brain (and likely yours, too) can focus longer once it's in a groove. It's frustrating when the timer stops the flow early.

Granted, if 25 minute gaps are all you can find, then it's better than nothing. Go for it.

It can be difficult to find these gaps as you start this process. That's exactly why professionals are forced to work on the weekends!

If you can't find any room for work blocks, why? Do you have too many meetings?

I'm going to challenge you to cut meetings significantly. Apply the problem-solving framework to your meeting-heavy schedule. Find solutions to buy back time.

You may need to add these stints into your schedule slowly.

Bucketing and planning your calendar according to area of responsibility forces you to see the gaps.

As mentioned earlier, leverage good stress to integrate the neglected buckets into your life. Add a goal, a deadline and accountability to be sure your schedule is well-rounded.

Make focused work blocks your priority. If you do this right, everything will have a place in your calendar to be done.

The actual tasks you'll do within each time block do not need to be determined when planning your week. Just confirm that you will focus on Bucket 1 here, Bucket 2 there and Bucket 3 between X:00 and X:00 on this day.

Focus, Repeat And Tweak As Required

When the time comes for a work block, turn off all notifications.

Create a ritual that signals to your brain that you're entering focused work mode. You could put on a special hat or walk backwards to your desk - whatever works!

Look at your Task Circle. Focus ONLY on one bucket.

Start at "A" and work your way through the priorities as indicated by the alphabet until the time block is complete.

Take a break. Energize. Get distracted! You NEED the break otherwise it defeats the purpose of the whole system.

Rinse and repeat as many times as you can each week.

I know I'm making it sound easy. I recognize it's not.

Doing this consistently requires a shift in your day-to-day patterns. Multiple habits may need to change.

One-hat-at-a-time, one-task-at-a-time thinking can be a challenge for those who love to bop all over their to-do list.

When you rise to the challenge, your output per hour will increase. Doing more in less time allows you to compress your workload into assigned hours.

When you achieve that, you will not only be able to Take Back Your Weekends, but take back your power and take back your life!

You can see this entire method in action in my online program that complements this book.

It's called Take Back Your Weekends and is found at TakeBackYourWeekends.com

BONUS: For $100 off the purchase price of my online program use the coupon code READER$100 ▪

COACHING QUESTIONS

Do a brain dump of all the tasks you need to do.

What are your areas of responsibility?

Look at your schedule. Where are your windows to book focused work blocks?

Remember your energy flow when mapping your week.

If you don't have windows of time in your schedule, apply the problem-solving framework to find a way to create blocks of time.

Want to see this in action? Go to TakeBackYourWeekends.com to enrol in my full online course. Use the coupon code: READER$100 to get $100 off the purchase price.

Looking for more direction? Check out my coaching and speaking services at AllisonGraham.co

TAKE BACK
YOUR WEEKENDS

—

I hope you are as passionate about my message as I am and can see the possibilities.

It took me a decade of hell to develop these concepts. It took years more to prove that they consistently make a difference in the lives of my clients.

It would be unfair to have you reach the last chapter (Congratulations!) and not share ways for you to go deeper with my message.

Before I share the last few stories I encourage you to continue this journey. Please consider this book step one.

Earlier I mentioned how I created a list of the 21 best tips to take control of your time.

Since you've made it to the end of this book, I'd love to share this with you for free!

Just go to TakeBackYourWeekends.com to gain access to those 21 tips and other reader bonuses!

Want even more? Connect with me on various social media platforms. I'm most active on Linked In. allisongraham.co/linkedin

Of course, a review of this book on Amazon will help others find the content. Feel free to share the link with anyone you believe would benefit. Thank you.

I believe there are people in the world who are stressed and suffering unnecessarily. They need this information.

They turn ice cubes into snowmen. They interpret obstacles as adversities and tasks as obstacles. They live in a state of constant stress and don't even realize that there is a better, less stressful way to do all they do.

You, on the contrary, are ahead of the game!

You now know why most stress is unnecessary.

You're empowered to choose a better, less stressful way.

This book has given you the mindset and methodology to experience less stress, do more and be happier.

Every time a reader or audience member sends me a note, I know my journey to develop this content was worth it!

Like the time when a professional sent me a letter. She said she got more practical value in one of my speeches than in nine years of therapy.

She finally understood why she's so stressed and unhappy and how to change that pattern.

Or the advisor who went through my Take Back Your Weekends online program.

She said, "I feel seen for the first time in a decade."

Later she told a group coaching class how powerful the program was because she became aware of her emotional response to client obstacles.

Her pattern had unknowingly been sucking enthusiasm out of her days for years. Now, she's working to interrupt that pattern to be less stressed.

The stories continue.

Each one represents a life that was touched by shifting their perspective on tasks, obstacles and adversities.

As I type this final paragraph, what's really on my mind is your story.

What path will you walk to Take Back Your Weekends? ▪

CPSIA information can be obtained
at www.ICGtesting.com
Printed in the USA
LVHW052358310521
689000LV00016B/1011